Led by the Spirit

*How the Holy Spirit guides
the believer*

Jim Elliff

press

Dundas, Ontario
1999

Joshua Press Inc., Dundas, Ontario
© 1999 by Joshua Press Inc.
Published 1999
Printed in Canada

Editorial director: Michael A.G. Haykin
Creative/production manager: Janice Van Eck

© Cover photography by Jacob Joseph, Dundas, Ontario

Scripture quotations taken from *The New King James Version*,
© 1991 by Thomas Nelson, Inc.

Canadian Cataloguing in Publication Data

Elliff, Jim, 1948–
    Led by the Spirit: how the Holy Spirit guides the believer

Rev. & expanded from "Led by the Spirit" originally published in
Reformation and revival journal, v. 3, no. 2, Spring 1994 and the
adapted version published by Christian Communicators
Worldwide, 1997.
ISBN 1-894400-00-3

1. Christian life. 2. God – Will. 3. Holy Spirit. I. Title

BV4501.2.E444 1999   248.4   C99-930816-5

Contents

Preface
A personal admission

An open Bible lay in my lap as the hours passed in the prayer room. I was connecting as I read, not exactly with the words but with the Lord.

It is hard to explain the way I was reading the Bible, but my pattern had developed over a considerable period of time. I would read with eyes glazed over, convinced that through the pages of the Bible I could have a mystical encounter with God. I was not overly concerned about the context or even the content of what I was reading, for my purpose was not to know the Bible's words but to be directed by hearing God speak through them.

This may sound contradictory. How could I find a word of direction from the Bible but not especially care about its content and context? The answer lies in the desires of a young man who desperately wanted to obey God in every detail of his life. I wanted the Spirit of God to speak to me through the Word but without the use of my reason. I was suspicious about the mind and its reasoning processes. I sought therefore to bypass my reason for a more direct communication from God.

It now surprises me that I often received what I was looking for. Somewhere in those many hours of trance-like stillness, I felt that I heard God, and I could often point to a text of Scripture, usually entirely devoid of context, which was my personal "word" of guidance. God had spoken. I could have no doubt about his "word" to me.

Despite those many years in which I sought to listen to God by this mystical means, I have now come to a new position on guidance by the Spirit that I believe comes much closer to the biblical norm. This small book gives you my change in thinking. I'm not prepared, however, to throw out everything gained by the previous years. I will rather try to dissect error from truth in the same way we remove a weed from the garden.

This system of direct communications from God that I sought at least led me to seek communion with God. This is not to be despised. Intimacy and communion with God is a high and noble pursuit. Paul sacrificed the loss of all things for such communion and knowledge (Philippians 3:8–10). If my more rational approach to decision-making and guidance excludes warm and loving fellowship with God *in a conscious way*, I have thrown out too much.

I must also thank God that my system for finding his will did not lead me over any cliffs where recovery was impossible. I firmly believe that God protected me from missing any major directives in my life out of sheer grace, which is what keeps any of us from disaster no matter what we believe. Others have not been so blessed. I believe adamantly that *God speaks* to men and women—it is the *way* he does it that is in question, not at all the fact that he does.

Jim Elliff
Kansas City, Missouri
March, 1999

1

Two ways

You may have reached for this book as a person needing guidance about some seemingly *impossible* decision. Perhaps you are at the end of yourself in trying to get this thing solved. In the barrage of recommended solutions, answers seem more distant than ever. In fact, in the process you may become somewhat philosophical about it all. Questions may harass you like these:

- Can God tell me exactly what it is I am to do?
- What freedoms do I have in making up my own mind?
- What is "God's voice"?
- If I fail to get it right, am I permanently out of step with God?

The confusion commonly comes from trying to conjecture just whose voice you are to follow. Are you to listen to the voice of your own mind, God's voice through some extraordinary revelation, or the voice of a mentor or friend? Must it be remarkable in the way it comes, or can it come as an unadorned process of rational thinking?

In my earlier years I majored on discerning God's will by waiting for spiritual impressions. By this I mean that I sought some direct subjective revelation from God to show me the way. I was set on this being the only adequate way to be led through life and often instructed others in my way of doing it. Therefore I have a special interest in helping you discern the truth about such an approach.

Some of you are broadly experienced in such a subjective approach to decision-making and you will be reading to see where I differ with it. The words, "God revealed to me" are well-used terms for you. Maybe you have been delighted with the success you have had and will find it hard to accept another viewpoint. I understand your insistence.

Others of you may have little experience with intangible spiritual impressions. So, I believe it is important that I take some time initially to reassure you that you are *already* being led by God's Spirit. I am sympathetic with the fact that your unique Christian background (and perhaps your non-Christian history) has a lot to do with how you approach this issue.

Suppose the concept of spiritual impressions has never been part of your experience, and your Christian leaders never spoke of "hearing God's voice" or of "receiving revelation" from God. Among some Christians you might be made to believe that you are spiritually inferior, under-taught, and backward. Some would believe that you have no hope of ever discovering God's will for your life. But is this necessarily true?

2

Moral guidance

> Therefore, brethren, we are debtors—not to the
> flesh, to live according to the flesh. For if you
> live according to the flesh you will die; but if by
> the Spirit you put to death the deeds of the
> body, you will live. *For as many as are led by the
> Spirit of God, these are sons of God* (Romans
> 8:12–14, emphasis mine).

The above passage from Romans 8 tells us there is a
kind of guidance that you *do* experience. Please read it
again. Paul is maintaining that everyone who is a genuine
believer is led by the Spirit *in some way*. Everybody!
Whether you are one whose experience with direct spiritual
impressions is legion, or one who has gotten none.

But what kind of leading does he have in mind?

Paul is describing the leadership of the Spirit as that
which affects the believer *morally*. Let me unpack this
rich passage for you.

In Romans 1 Paul makes sure we understand that the
outright pagan is morally corrupt. Then, in Romans 2 he
shows us how the mere moralist (in this case, the unconverted
Jew) is also depraved or, as he puts it, "in the

flesh." In Romans 3 Paul can thus assert that "there is none righteous, no, not one" and that "all have sinned and fall short of the glory of God" (verses 10,23). The solution to this problem of universal sinfulness is God's giving his Son to die for sinners (Romans 5:6–8). Thus, in Romans 8 Paul can talk about those who have embraced by faith God's saving work as those who are "in the Spirit." They have been brought to a relationship of trust in Christ and to liberation from the law as the means of saving them.

On the other hand, he describes those who are seeking salvation through their own works or merits as being "in the flesh." Living legalistically or in this "flesh" way of trying to obey God's laws, actually is said to excite or bring forward all kinds of additional sins.

> When the commandment came, sin revived and I died....For sin, taking occasion by the commandment, deceived me, and by it killed *me*....sin, that it might appear sin, was producing death in me through what is good, so that sin through the commandment might become exceedingly sinful (Romans 7:9b,11,13b).

But now that you are in Christ, having dropped the "effort" approach to being converted, you are in the Spirit and freed from the law as a means of justifying yourself before God. The effect of this is that you are now a person who puts "to death the deeds of the body." That is, if you are led by the Spirit, your nature is changed from the old person you used to be. And one of the climactic changes has to do with the new dominating power of the Spirit at work in you in putting away sins and destroying evil desires—a power you never had before, even if you were a moralist.

The passage says that it is "by the Spirit" that all of this happens. He guides the believer into this loving obedience that so brands his life from now on. It is the Spirit who creates a disinclination for the "deeds of the body" and a love for what is pure. It is the Spirit who enables the Christian to battle perseveringly against sin and fulfill his or her spiritual obligations. How does the Spirit do this?

3

God's inside work

> Therefore, my beloved, as you have always
> obeyed, not as in my presence only, but now
> much more in my absence, work out your own
> salvation with fear and trembling; for it is God
> who works in you both to will and to do for *His*
> good pleasure (Philippians 2:12–13).

The Word of God teaches that the Spirit does this work
of sanctification (the working out of our *daily* salvation
or deliverance from sin), not by direct inner impressions
or "voices," but by working within the mind and affections of the person. He changes our thinking by "working in us to will and to do of his good pleasure"
(Philippians 2:13). There is no doubt that in this process
of change *we* are the ones who are using our *wills* and *we*
are the ones *doing*. But at the same time it is *God* who is
"working" inside our minds to accomplish his ultimate
"good pleasure." Jonathan Edwards (1703–1758), the
New England pastor-theologian, spoke of this truth in
this way: "God produces all, and we act all, for that's
what God produces—our own acts."

The writer of Hebrews asserts the non-mystical nature

of this guidance when he reports that God has said: "I will put My laws in their *mind* and write them on their *hearts*" (8:10b, emphasis mine). By his Holy Spirit, God has come into the life of the Christian with rightness. The believer is now constituted as one who loves and demonstrates that rightness—not absolutely, of course, but substantively, even though he or she still lives in a fallen body.

Even the statement of Christ in John 10:27 ("My sheep hear My voice, and I know them, and they follow Me") is a metaphor of the assumed communion between the believer and Christ that leads the believer into a lifestyle of obedience. Here Christ is not saying that every believer has a life of mystical experiences of God. Rather, he is speaking of the normal experience of all of his sheep who have genuine fellowship with him. Such an experience involves a *following* of Christ in definite obedience.

This view does not insist that the work of the Spirit should be termed anti-supernatural. Such moral guidance is *decidedly* supernatural. But it is not required to be unusual and direct, as if it happens without the mind and apart from reason.

If we say, therefore, that every real Christian is led by God in this way, as these verses do, we are certainly not *requiring* anything mystical in that leadership at all.

Genuine believers who do not have a long list of mystical experiences of guidance to report can thus take heart. You have not been forgotten by God nor are you second-class Christians in any respect, but you are among those who are authentic *followers* of the Lord Jesus. You are being led by the Spirit!

4

A work of grace

This moral guidance is seen in a variety of ways. The authentic believer has a living interaction with the Scriptures, both in his delight in them and in his experience of being rebuked by them. As David said, "I will delight myself in Your statutes; I will not forget Your word" (Psalm 119:16).

When you read and take the Scriptures to heart, for instance; or when you are reminded of the dictates of Scripture during times of temptation; or when you reason morally about temptation itself; or when you find your affections turned to righteousness and against your former sins (even when others are not looking)—it is in times like these that you are experiencing the activity of the Spirit leading you into practical righteousness.

The non-Christian has an intensely different view of God's authority. Whether or not he is religious, he ultimately prefers his own authority to God's, therefore choosing to live as an enemy of God and his commands. As the Apostle Paul puts it: "the carnal [unregenerate] mind is enmity against God; for it is not subject to the law of God, nor indeed can be" (Romans 8:7).

Why is it that true believers experience a type of conviction with regard to sin that has to do with all aspects of morality? They are just as certainly concerned about being overpaid a small amount of change at the cash register as they are of consciously defrauding on their income tax. Their agonies and their joys often stem from how they respond to this guidance of the Spirit. This "universal" obedience (meaning that it affects all aspects of life of which the believer is knowledgeable) is the work of the Holy Spirit who *has* changed them and who *is* changing them and guiding them.

What I am seeking to convey is that there is a guidance which has everything to do with grace and the work of the Spirit within us. Yes, there is truth and there is counsel, and there is circumstance, but if we are guided *morally* it is because of a new way of thinking and new affections in the subterranean river of our redeemed minds. We are morally different because the Spirit indwelling us makes us different. I am asserting that *God* does this and it is distinctly a matter of grace operating in the mind and affections of every true believer.

I find this leadership, this inner moral tutelage and superintendence, a liberating certainty. I am occupied by God and morally checked by God's Spirit at work in my thinking. I may chafe against this leadership at times, but the persistent and loving pressure of it eventually wins—so much so that the Romans 8:12–14 verses are true for me. I am eventually overcome by the grace of the Spirit! I cannot live comfortably without such obedience and conformity to this Spirit-induced thinking, nor can I ultimately divorce myself from it.

So we have started with what is certain—you are a

guided Christian in this most important sphere of morality. Let me take you a step beyond moral guidance into an additional certainty by opening up another area of guidance which is part and parcel of the experience of every Christian.

5

Guidance into truth

However when He, the Spirit of truth, has
come, *He will guide you into all truth*; for He will
not speak on His own authority, but whatever
He hears He will speak; and He will tell you
things to come. He will glorify Me, for He will
take of what is Mine and declare it to you. All
things that the Father has are Mine. Therefore
I said that He will take of Mine and declare it to
you (John 16:13–15, emphasis mine).

Here, the Lord Jesus speaks of another aspect of guidance,
guidance into *truth*. This promise of guidance by the
Spirit was given initially to the Apostles to whom he spoke
these words and had to do with their writing down of what
we know as the New Testament. Yet, there is a secondary
application of these words to every true believer. Jesus
said, "If you abide in My word [meaning to remain under
its moral persuasion or to consistently obey it], you are My
disciples indeed. And you shall know the truth, and the
truth shall make you free" (John 8:31b,32). No one can be
Christ's disciple without this obedience to his Word. And
the result of this obedience to the Word is that the real dis-

ciple will be led into more truth—a liberating truth indeed!

Did not Paul refer to every true believer when he said: "Now we have received, not the spirit of the world, but the Spirit who is from God, that we might know the things that have been freely given to us by God" (1 Corinthians 2:12)? Others outside of the Christian fold cannot understand them, "because they are spiritually discerned" (1 Corinthians 2:14). This guidance of the Spirit into truth is also what Christ was surely referring to when he said that his sheep never follow the voice of a stranger (John 10:5).

Guidance into truth is carried out in the way Jesus expressed to his disciples in John 14:26: "But the Helper, the Holy Spirit, whom the Father will send in My name, He will teach you all things, and bring to your remembrance all things that I said to you." This is the two-fold manifestation of truth to the believer. First, the Holy Spirit *instructs* the mind. Second, he *reminds* or brings to remembrance. Again, it is the person who has the ability, the genuine capacity, to understand and cling to truth who is the undoubted recipient of this guidance.

And in John's first letter, we are told that Christians have a permanent anointing, which is none other than the Holy Spirit, and "you do not need that anyone teach you; but as the same anointing teaches you concerning all things, and is true, and is not a lie, and just as it has taught you, you will abide in Him" (1 John 2:27). John cannot mean that we are to avoid being taught by men, for he himself is teaching them through his letter. Rather, he means that this unique knowledge, this capacity to know and embrace truth, is a gift of the Holy Spirit within the believer and is not at all found in others outside the Body of Christ.

6

Unable to see

There is an interesting subtheme in the Gospel of John. As you read through the book, you notice the profound inability of the Pharisees to grasp the truth of Jesus' teaching. Their inability to comprehend the meaning of his coming and so find salvation is ultimately seen in their final rejection of him and their willing infliction of death on him as if he were a common criminal. As Jesus himself said to them:

> Why do you not understand My speech? Because you are not able to listen to My word....And if I tell the truth, why do you not believe Me? He who is of God hears God's words; therefore you do not hear, because you are not of God (John 8:43,46b,47).

Later, in John 10, Jesus says this to these blind guides of the blind:

> I told you, and you do not believe. The works that I do in My Father's name, they bear witness of Me. But you do not believe, because you are not of My sheep, as I said to you. My sheep hear My voice, and I know them, and they follow Me (John 10:25–27).

Many Christians carry the blindness of non-belief too far, believing that persons outside of Christ could not possibly state the basic views of Christianity. But this is not true.

A friend of mine once went to a lecture given by a famous professor of classics at the University of Toronto. This professor's expertise lay in the field of early Christianity. He had written and lectured widely in this field, covering such topics as the life and thought of Tertullian, the famous North African theologian, and the way that the reign of Constantine (died A.D. 337) impacted the church of his day. Now, if you listened to this man lecture or if you read his books, you might have thought him to be a Christian, for he was able to state perfectly the core beliefs and doctrines of Christianity. In reality, though, he was an atheist. One could well imagine him after a lecture thinking to himself, "I will never be found following such a system of belief!" He may think he understands Christianity, but the truth of the matter is that he really does not understand even though he thinks he does. For if the reality of Christ were actually known to him, he would be following after him.

All ultimate truth *demands* embracing by its very nature. This professor does not understand hell or he would seek to escape it. He does not understand Christ's offer of eternal life and heaven, or he would capitulate to him. Rather, he actually believes these views to be a lie. Are we to say that he understands Christianity if he perceives it to be a lie? But, on the other hand, *you* have capitulated precisely because you do understand (see Matthew 13:1–23).

Jesus used the Old Testament Scriptures to enforce this concept when he said:

> It is written in the prophets, *'And they shall all be taught by God.'* Therefore everyone who has heard and learned from the Father comes to Me (John 6:45).

So the work of the Spirit is that which you as a believer have already enjoyed. There is really nothing mystical about it. It is going on by virtue of the Spirit's indwelling in conjunction with his already revealed Word. This understanding of the truth as it is found in Scripture is called illumination, and does not bypass the processes of the mind at all. Teaching presupposes the mental process; being reminded assumes the same. If you are a true believer, you may say with confidence, "I am guided by the Spirit into truth." As in the case of moral guidance, this guidance into truth is definitional—it defines the nature of the Christian.

But now we must move on into the third aspect of guidance, an area in which we are not nearly as confident as the other aspects of guidance we have been considering. This is the guidance that the Spirit gives in non-moral issues, guidance about concerns not directly informed by Scripture. It concerns such things as:

- Shall I engage in this business?
- Which school should I go to?
- What car should I buy?

7

Illuminism

How do you respond to this question, "Just how does God lead the believer in these matters of personal concern for which there is no detailed biblical information or instruction?" Evangelicals respond in such variety to this question that many believers are often left in a quandary. Notable among these numerous answers is what we may call "illuminism" (to be distinguished from illumination, where the Spirit opens up the mind to the meaning of the biblical text). The illuminist seeks guidance from God by getting a series of impressions, which he believes come as God directly impacts his spirit.

The illuminist is often wary of the mind and using his or her reason. Certainly we need to be cautious lest we fall into the error of blindly trusting bare unaided reason. The illuminist, though, often goes so far as to reject any hope that reason can be useful. "This doesn't come from me," he will say, "it comes from God."

The noble Count Nikolaus Ludwig von Zinzendorf (1700–1760) and his fellow Moravians were at this place when the Count founded what was called "A Society of Little Fools." He wrote that the members "were not to use their own brains; they were to wish they had no brains; they were to be like little children in arms."[1] It is not surprising that the Moravians went on to practice such strange customs as opening the pages of the Bible at random for guidance.

Personally I have a genuine appreciation for the intentions of many sincere illuminists. For one thing, they take seriously the immanence of God. To them God is never far removed from the human condition, no distant Landlord. They hunger for the demonstration of God's power and life in their midst, both for their own joy (not at all a bad motive, see John 16:24) and the witness it affords to others.

When I lived in this kind of practice myself, I found much excitement and anticipation. I was deeply sincere. As far as I could tell, my aim was God's glory. I am sure that God values the heart and faith of many sincere illuminists. And, as I will say again, I am sure that he sometimes blesses them—though for reasons other than their method of guidance.

On the other end of the spectrum is the cold intellectualist. To such a person the only way that God now deals with human beings is through the pathway of reason, but it is an unsubmissive and untrusting reason. To them God's work in the universe is accomplished primarily, if not solely, through various natural laws, such as the law of gravity, which are discoverable by reason. In the eighteenth century such a view was called Deism and was rightly shunned by Evangelicals as sub-biblical.

Just how does God speak? Interestingly, the Bible answers our question by showing that God speaks in any way he wants! God has guided men and women in history not only with deep impressions, but also with the casting of lots, "fleeces," angelic visitations, visions, inner burdens, the recalling of Bible prophecy, cosmic signs, prophetic utterances, dreams, theophanies, and so on. He has been very creative in his communications.

From the experience and text of Scripture alone it might then be assumed that the average child of God will always or at least often be guided in these more or less direct and dynamic ways. But is this assumption correct?

8

Direct interventions

Let me express my growing understanding of direct interventions that bypass reason in three statements or theses:

Direct communication by God for personal guidance is not commanded by Scripture nor is there any implication that it is part and parcel of what is the normal Christian life—on the other hand, such guidance is not ruled out.

We have seen that the guidance of the Spirit through the mind toward a life of obedience and toward truth is propounded in Scripture as essential Christianity. Nowhere though does the Bible teach that direct guidance by means of impressions *must* be the experience of the believer. Those who argue that such experiences are to be regular fare for the Christian virtually always make their case on the basis of the narrative or story sections of the Bible and not on those that are didactic or teaching sections.

I have not been told by God in his Word that divine visitations of unusual nature constitute authentic Christianity. I have not been commanded to have them or seek them. Interestingly enough, Christ himself said that it is an evil and adulterous generation that seeks a sign (Matthew 12:39). But this lack of intimation and command does not logically rule out the possibility of receiving peculiar impulses from God.

Except in rare cases, the experience of direct interventions of God's guidance in the lives of various Bible characters was not indicative of normal discipleship and they are likely recorded precisely because of their unusual nature.

Due to the compressed makeup of the Bible it appears to its reader that God is speaking directly more often than he actually does. Abraham had some direct discussions with God, but they were few and far between. Noah got his word from God and hammered away for many, many years without much else being said. Paul was a man of many revelations (2 Corinthians 12:1–10), yet this was a sign of his unique calling as a Bible author and apostle and is nowhere given as a standard—rather, he is a notable exception among men. Just as the reality of miracles is abused by making it normative ("Expect a miracle every day!"), so the work of direct revelation is discredited by reducing it to the common. John the Baptist, we must remember, did no sign (see John 10:41).

If God does impress us with directives outside of Scripture, we still have nothing sure.

If I sense God speaking to me in a way apart from Scripture, I need not rule it out. God may do that. He has done that in the past, and he can do what he wishes. But I am still without final assurance that it is his voice. I must use my reason and knowledge of Scripture to test what I feel I am hearing.

How do I know that I have heard God directly? Illuminists have elaborate answers for this. They may say that he speaks in a still, small voice, but did he do that on Mt. Sinai? God speaks in a way that is not demanding they may say. But does he always? They may say that they know it is of God by the unusual way in which it came. Or they may say that the impression is accompanied by certain feelings (peace, harmony, humility, love, etc.). But there are no such instructions in the Bible about how such criteria are determinative in discerning God's voice. In the final analysis illuminists have no way of knowing if what they have received is of God or not. In fact, the greatest deviations from Christianity in the last two centuries were begun with similar private revelations.

9

Assurance for the illuminist

In my own earlier experience as an illuminist I used to resort to saying, "I know that I know that I know." That phrase was not original, but it expressed that I felt the only way to know if my supposed revelation was from God was that it was accompanied by its own assurance. It at least left people without argument against me. If I knew, then I knew.

After many years in a measure of sincere illuminism, I came to realize that only about half of my impressions appeared to have some possible validity. I probably could have guessed at least that well! In addition, I noticed that decisions made between illuminists often were locked up by differing revelations, sometimes quite contrary!

I am not saying that God never spoke to me, but only that I had no real assurance that I had heard him speak. I could prove nothing. My experience of hearing God's voice was not any more verifiable than that of the prominent faith healer who said God told him that he would take the faith healer's life if people did not give a certain amount of money for one of the man's projects. There is no essential difference. The illuminist chooses to believe that what he experiences is true, and this is all he can say. His revelation is entirely self-authenticating.

A particular brand of illuminism has seemingly answered the problem of assurance by seeking the "word" from God through the actual Scripture text. By this method the Bible is read, sometimes consecutively, until the Spirit impresses a passage or phrase to the reader in such a way that it is said to be "given" to him. The reader may say, "This is what this means to me." Often these verses are wrenched out of context or are interpreted in a way that is not known to anyone else but that individual. But did God author the Scripture for merely private interpretation?

Gilbert K. Chesterton (1874–1936), the well-known Christian apologist who delighted in using paradox to promote the truth, once said, and I am paraphrasing, "A person should be careful of reading his own Bible until he can read everyone else's." In other words, an entirely individual use of the Bible is at best wrong and at worst dangerous.

I am embarrassed to say that I almost got married on this basis! On a certain occasion I read in Jeremiah 31:22b, "The Lord has created a new thing in the earth— a woman shall encompass a man." A female friend had surprised me by relating her conviction that it was God's will for her to marry me. I proceeded to wrongly interpret this verse as my having been "encompassed" or "surrounded." I was serious about obeying, but my interpretation was entirely mystical and private. Though the woman I was considering was certainly godly, I am convinced (and later, she was convinced) that I was right in this case not to follow my "heavenly vision."

10

The testimony of a genuine man of faith

George Müller (1805–1898), the man who fed and clothed over 10,000 orphans without asking for a penny from anyone but God and believed that God had granted over 50,000 answers to his prayers, is often falsely cited as using Scripture in the way of the illuminist. Being a student of Müller's life and writings I can say unreservedly that he did not.[2] In fact, he would have strongly refused to take any Scripture verse out of context.

Müller is noted for the stating of his *reasons* for particular actions in his journals. His setting out of these reasons indicates that he was no mystic. Granted, certain verses of Scripture were pointed out to him by the Holy Spirit, and God made them life-texts, but in every one of them the meaning would be the same to anyone who read it. Consider the following quotes:

> Impressions have neither one thing nor the other to do with faith. Faith has to do with the Word of God. It is not impressions, strong or weak, which will make the difference. We have to do with the Written Word

and not ourselves or our impressions.[3]

> Faith has nothing to do with feelings or with impressions, with improbabilities or with outward experiences. If we desire to couple such things with faith, then we are no longer resting on the Word of God, because faith needs nothing of the kind. Faith rests on the naked Word of God. When we take Him at His Word, the heart is at peace.[4]

We can say that all of the promises of God intended for believers under the new covenant established by Jesus Christ are ours without exception. Yet we should pray for faith to believe them. God, who gives differing measures of faith, may grant a person the ability to trust him on the basis of that promise to a greater degree than he does others. He may certainly emphasize a verse, but what we need is faith, not impressions about verses out of context.

The Bible used in the illuminist's way is reduced to no more value in terms of guidance than a phone book or an advertisement on a billboard. The meaning is thrown out the window. Would the Holy Spirit, who authored the Scriptures for the purpose of their being our infallible guide, promote them as a grab-bag of all kinds of meanings?

Mysticism in the area of guidance casts doubt on the adequacy of Scripture (2 Timothy 3:16–17). It is interesting to note that mysticism and liberalism often become bedfellows. In some current waves of mysticism, precisely in the areas we are talking about, those without a sound view of the inerrancy of Scripture find just as much freedom to be illuminists as those who are Evangelicals. At a minimum, illuminism takes our eyes away from the Scriptures and focuses them on our own personal experience. A creeping liberalism is to be expected as a lamentable end result of the pursuit of inner revelations. The Evangelical who believes the Bible is God's infallible Word, yet is compelled to *really believe it* only when sensing some inner impression, is not far from the liberalism he despises. He demeans the adequacy of Scripture.

11

Distaste for reason

During the fading stages of the Great Awakening in the eighteenth century a mystical kind of "enthusiasm" or fanaticism sprang up. That which had been unusual and of rare occurrence was now expected as normative. In his *An Inquiry Into Enthusiasm* Benjamin Doolittle (1695–1749) of Northfield, Massachusetts, defined enthusiasm as "strong Fancy, Imagination or Conceit of having large Communications from or Participations with the Deity." He said it produces the following in those who practice it:

> (1) a contempt for all reason and argument, (2) faith without foundation, (3) blind obedience to impulses and "heated imaginations," (4) great and sudden joy, (5) contempt of all not wholly in sympathy with their position, and (6) a spirit of persecution against all who differ, to the limit of their power; yet they will "bawl out Persecution, as loud as they can roar" if the "least Restraint" be put upon them.[5]

Concerning these divine impulses Ebenezer Morton, a layman from Middleboro, Massachusetts, penned this quaint poetry:

> Whate'er Men speak by this New-Light
> Still they are sure to be in the right:
> 'Tis a dark Lanthorn of a Spirit
> Which none see by but those that bear it:
> A Light that falls down from on high
> For Spiritual Trades to cozen by:
> An *Ignis Fatuus* that bewitches,
> And leads Men into Pools and Ditches.[6]

Illuminists tend to have a distaste for reason altogether. Yet how can we describe wisdom apart from reason? Wisdom is a process of cognition, not a bombshell out of the sky. In our non-thinking day it is quite popular to short-cut the painful process of reasoning for a blank waiting on some inner voice. It seems highly spiritual to do so and carries with it a magical authority. ("I got this from God at four o'clock in the morning!") In this way the most spiritually unkempt believer or the novice has equal voice with the wisest Christian veteran.

We must admit that interest in mysticism among Evangelicals is increasingly influenced by our culture. One wonders how much this desire to be mystical is only the Christian expression of that New Age mysticism flourishing in the non-Christian world around us. Increasingly our world is short on thinking and long on experience. Mix this with inner turmoil and a desperate need for answers from some higher source, along with the infiltration of eastern religions, and you can easily see why the mystical aspects of our culture are so predominant. Our generation would certainly far rather load all of their information in a computer and forget the agony of thinking, especially thinking biblically.

In all that I have said about this illuministic approach to guidance, I want to assert again that nothing is implied about the believer's motives being insincere. Nor have I said that God cannot send a Divine impulse to the believer involved in this way of finding guidance. Yet I am certainly saying that our lack of assurance as to its source casts us back on sanctified reasoning.

God may use the sincere individual who gets his guidance the illuminist's way. He may bless him. He may honour his faith more than his method. I am quite sure that God always condescends to our imperfections. And if there is immaturity, we must realize that God will often use in our zealous immaturity what he disallows in our maturity.

The Great Awakening preacher, George Whitefield (1714–1770), who had such tendencies in his earlier days, later commented, "I am a man of like passions with others, and consequently may have sometimes mistaken nature for grace, imagination for revelation."[7] He put away his illuministic patterns as he grew in Christ. Yet, it is important to note that he was used in those earlier days just as dramatically as in later life.

12

Interpreting impressions

Christians should be very humble about this matter of hearing God's voice. If, in some unusual manner, the Spirit gives a direct impression, we should say, "I believe that God is speaking to me in a special inner way about all of this, but I must test this out carefully by other means to know for sure."

Unfortunately, there are some Christian groups which do not allow for humility or tentativeness in this area. They say that true faith is known by the bold declaration of the impression you have been given. Thus the one speaking runs the danger of declaring what God has not said, which is strictly prohibited in Deuteronomy 18:20. I find this a sad bondage. I am certain that some express themselves so forthrightly about their revelations so as to help convince themselves that what they think they heard is actually so. Nonetheless, it is not safe, especially when it concerns directions for others' lives.

You may remember the car full of unclothed religious extremists picked up in a southern American town a few years ago. Their leader supposedly had some very specific knowledge imparted to him from God that they were to get in their vehicle and go, taking *nothing* with them at all.

I distrust both their literalism and their illuminism! Although this illustration is a bit far removed from most of us, the basis for its credibility is no different than that of anyone else who says he hears God.

Some of the early Quakers in the seventeenth century were also known to have stripped naked before Protestant audiences—they called it "going naked as a sign"!—under supposed guidance from the "inner light."[8] There would be very few Evangelicals today who would not think that they were misguided. And yet would not the Quakers have been able to point to a "word" from Isaiah for an example of going naked (Isaiah 20:1–2)?

In addition to all I have said about the Word and sanctified reason playing the vital part in guidance, one needs to remember that the Christian's reasoning is unlike the world's (see 1 Corinthians 2:6–8). I have often been, to my knowledge, impressed to speak to someone about Christ. Upon submitting that thought to sanctified reason I am often still compelled to do so. To the non-believer, speaking to a stranger in the airport about Christ may seem irrational. To the believer, who works with wisdom from better premises, the action is entirely reasonable. We are to be compassionate about the state of others and we are to be bold and ready to witness for Christ. So we are to be biblically rational, though not rationalistic. This is not a subtle raising of reason above God. Rather, it is a recognition that normally God works through reason.

At times what is perceived as being a rather direct impression of God is really nothing other than the store of accumulated Scripture knowledge coming to bear on your thinking. Without being able to fully express just why you believe you should take a course of action, you are being led by years of Bible knowledge converging on the subject. You understand the "ways of God."

Moses certainly had exceptional revelatory experiences beyond even the prophets (see Numbers 12:6–8), but he also knew the ways of God—"He made known His ways to Moses, His acts to the children of Israel" (Psalm 103:7). This is the normative leadership of the Holy Spirit, which we have already looked at, and who will, we are told, "bring to your remembrance all things that I said to you" (John 14:26b).

What fills me with foreboding is the possibility for grand delusions if sanctified reasoning is not given its proper place. We are seeing a massive world-view shift in our society with increased emphasis on the supernatural. Sometimes voices are heard, or help is given by so-called spirit guides who communicate through human mediums. If Evangelicals are building their faith on a foundation of phenomena and experiences rather than on a base of truth, what will be the outcome? And what essential difference is there between these voices?

13

Sanctifying reason

Much of the argument in this book has been linked to what I have called "sanctified reason." What does this term mean? As you have seen, I am rooted to the position that reason and Scripture are systemic and essential to sound decision-making. I am not constrained to limit God's activity to that alone—God can do as he wishes—but the rational approach is the normal way.

We are to actually think through the given situation, wrestle with the options, weigh them, sift them, ponder the implications and consequences, and we are to do all of this in the light of truth as we find it in the Scriptures interpreted in context. And we presume, underneath all of this, God is working.

But if reason is unaided, if it is *mere* reason by itself, it will do little good. Reason standing alone might lead us to some sort of workable resolution, but it carries the liability of doing so without pleasing God. That circumstance is as unsatisfying to us as it is unsatisfactory to God.

God is always and only pleased with faith (Hebrews 11:6). To sanctify our reasoning process is to yield to his infinite wisdom and to expect from him every ounce of help that is necessary to make a decision that is both wise and pleasing to him. If faith is anything it is an *attentive* and *conscious* recognition of God's place in all the details of life.

We are to deliberately place our rational faculties at the feet of God. In the same way that one walks out of one room and into another, believers are told to "come before his presence" (Psalm 95:2). By this the writers of the Bible intend to convey that there is a "manifested presence" of God, which is that nearness of God that is experienced or felt. Lovers of God should not be satisfied with only the bare fact that God is everywhere, but should seek his face. And we must do so with an open Bible.

It is true that God works in us "to will and to do," but this is no excuse for failing to consciously bring our thoughts captive to God—rather, for the believer, the undercurrent of the Spirit's work within us is seen to be the very reason we will do so.

It is part of loving the Lord with all of your mind (see Mark 12:30) and setting your mind on the things above (see Colossians 3:2) for the Christian to habituate himself to thinking his thoughts after God's. However, in the case of determining just exactly what God would have us do in a *specific* matter, there is motive to be even more intentional about it.

Placing a matter before God so as to seek his presence and to rest in his intervention, is to greatly reduce the options before us. While waiting on God, we often find that God simplifies our choices. There have been many times that I have come to him with a discomfiting jumble of options only to find that spending some period in his presence reduces my selection down to just two—

and then, one. I am thinking out my thoughts before God, sometimes with a list of pros and cons, under the brilliant floodlight of the Word. Müller had something to say about the way that God works:

> God guides, not by a visible sign, but by swaying the judgment. To wait before Him, weighing candidly in the scales every consideration for or against a proposed course, and in readiness to see which way the preponderance lies, is a frame of mind and heart in which one is fitted to be guided; and God touches the scales and makes the balance to sway as He will. But our hands must be off the scales, otherwise we need expect no interposition of His in our favor.[9]

The hazards of becoming a mere rationalist are obvious. You must be as vigilant to avoid running aground on that sandbar as you are of being swept over the waterfall of mysticism. The guided believer recognizes the decided value of appropriately relating to Christ and not just assuming, in a casual way, the blessing of God on his thinking. You *need* God. And the Father is far more likely to help you when you recognize the fundamental issue of your total poverty of thought apart from him.

You are not an independent thinker anymore. That describes your old life. Now you are to be a God-saturated and Scripture-oriented thinker.

14

The normative approach

We must live in the spirit of prayer to be guided believers in these non-moral areas. There is no gain if we operate, as it were, by natural unassisted reason, but there is every hope for wisdom if we genuinely rely on the Holy Spirit to supply it. God delights in those who seek to live the life of faith. And God wants it to be said that it was he who supplied the wisdom. Therefore we must *ask*.

> If any of you lacks wisdom, let him ask of God, who gives to all liberally and without reproach, and it will be given to him. But let him ask in faith, with no doubting, for he who doubts is like a wave of the sea driven and tossed by the wind. For let not that man suppose that he will receive anything from the Lord; *he is* a double-minded man, unstable in all his ways (James 1:5–8).

Again it was George Müller who once said that nine-tenths of knowing God's will has to do with "having no will of our own." A concerted effort to rid ourselves of selfish desires as they relate to our decision is foundational. Then, after and during prayer, another look at the will must be taken.

Taking into due consideration all of the normal helps for the believer—good counsel from godly friends, one's circumstances, godly priorities, any boundaries of Scripture, knowledge of the "ways" of God—the believer will be led to a way of thinking about the issue at hand. If he is perfectly willing to do anything, what does he *now* desire? After all, God is pleased to give him those desires.

> Delight yourself also in the Lord, and He shall give you the desires of your heart. Commit your way to the Lord, trust also in Him, and He shall bring it to pass (Psalm 37:4–5).

Such a thoughtful, biblically-induced attraction toward certain holy desires, with patient waiting before God in prayer, is no less the work of the Spirit than the most dramatic "immediate impulse" others may claim. This is the normal biblical pathway to wisdom. The man who makes the wise decision, yet always remains open to God's further intervention in whatever way God pleases, is demonstrating normative spiritual guidance.

The contemporary Reformed theologian J. I. Packer provides summary insight with this clarifying quote:

> God's guidance is more like the marriage guidance, child guidance, or career guidance that is received from counselors than it is like being "talked down" by the airport controller as one flies blind through the clouds. Seeking God's guidance is not like practicing divination or consulting oracles, astrologers, and clairvoyants for information about the future,

but rather is comparable with everyday thinking through of alternative options in given situations to determine the best course open to us. The inward experience of being divinely guided is not ordinarily one of seeing signs or hearing voices, but rather one of being enabled to work out the best thing to do.[10]

15

A strategy

To group together in a practical way some of the previous thoughts, let me suggest the following as a helpful list to consider when seeking God's will in matters of guidance. I would suggest that you look on this as a cluster of thoughts rather than an exact methodology or approach.

- Begin by prayer for wisdom. Do not doubt that God has a wise course of action for you and will make it known.

- Intentionally seek God's face even more than his answers. "In Your light we see light." (Psalm 36:9)

- Seek to be willing to take any course that God would have for you. Be thorough in your work on yourself. Often people miss God's will because they are not fully willing to be submissive to God *whatever* he leads them to do.

- Carefully seek to discover if there are any directives already given in Scripture which could guide you. Are there illustrations, commands, principles, which speak to this issue? Meditate on these and see if

Scripture promotes or rules out any action you are considering. Try to find not only what God permits and does not permit, but what God likes, what is dear to his heart. Go directly to any passage which deals with the general subject to see if there is help to be found which you had not discovered before. Always read the Bible in context.

- List each possible course of action, and in a prayerful frame of mind write out what are the pros and cons of each option. Put these options before the lens of Scripture one by one to see if God has spoken on these issues in some way. You will find more being said about most issues than you might first believe.

- When helpful, seek objective counsel from godly and wise men or women you can trust.

- Finally, examine your will again. If you are willing to do anything God might direct and that is certain in your mind, then you are free to pursue what God may be placing in your thinking related to the issue. Is there a long-term righteous desire in you?

- Now, act in faith. If God in his perfect cadence intervenes so as to cause everything to turn again, this is his business. For your part, you are required to take action along the lines of the wisest choice you can possibly make. Rejoice and do God's will!

Endnotes

[1] R. A. Knox, *Enthusiasm. A Chapter in the History of Religion* (Oxford: Clarendon Press, 1950), 413–414.

[2] For a list of verses that Müller held dear because they contained promises from God, see Arthur Pierson, *George Müller of Bristol* (Old Tappan, New Jersey: Revell, n.d.), 377–385. It is noteworthy that Müller took none of these texts out of context.

[3] Quoted Miles Stanford, *Principles of Spiritual Growth* (Lincoln, Nebraska: Back to the Bible, 1972), 8.

[4] Quoted William Henry Harding, *The Life of George Müller* (Westwood, New Jersey: Barbour, 1985), 372.

[5] Quoted Edwin Scott Gaustad, *The Great Awakening in New England* (New York: Harper & Brothers, 1957), 78.

[6] Quoted *ibid.*, 77–78.

[7] Knox, *Enthusiasm*, 450.

[8] For an excellent study of this phenomenon, see Kenneth L. Carroll, "Early Quakers and 'Going Naked as a Sign'," *Quaker History*, 67 (1978), 69–87.

[9] Pierson, *George Müller*, 185–186.

[10] *Hot Tub Religion* (Wheaton, Illinois: Tyndale House Publishers, 1987), 117–118.

Designed by Janice Van Eck
Set in ITC Dyadis and Janson Text
Printed by Annan & Sons, Toronto